WEIGHT TRAINING FOR YOUNG ATHLETES

DR. FRANCO COLUMBU
WITH R.R. KNUDSON

Contemporary Books, Inc.
Chicago

Library of Congress Cataloging in Publication Data

Columbu, Franco.
  Weight training for young athletes.

    Includes Index.
    SUMMARY: Discusses the benefits of weight lifting
in improving muscular fitness and strength and offers
instruction in basic weight lifting techniques.
    1. Weight lifting—Juvenile literature.   [1. Weight
lifting]   II. Knudson, R. Rozanne, 1932-
joint author.   III. Title.
GV546.C65   796.4'1   78-31696
ISBN 0-8092-7479-5
ISBN 0-8092-7478-7 pbk.

Published by Contemporary Books, Inc.
180 North Michigan Avenue, Chicago, Illinois 60601
Manufactured in the United States of America
Library of Congress Catalog Card Number: 78-31696
International Standard Book Number: 0-8092-7479-5 (cloth)
                                   0-8092-7478-7 (paper)

Published simultaneously in Canada by
Beaverbooks, Ltd.
150 Lesmill Road
Don Mills, Ontario M3B 2T5
Canada

In loving memory of
ALEX BUSEK

Contents

1

Muscles

This is a book about muscles, yours and mine.

It's about how our muscles work. And about how I can help you make your muscles work better.

Even at your young age you've probably spent a lot of time thinking about your body. You have certain favorite parts of it. Maybe you have unusually long fingers, which come in handy when you grab a football for passing. Long fingers control the football. Or maybe you're tall for a boy your age. Those extra inches help you score points in basketball. And during baseball season you make the most of your excellent eyesight. Good eyes can tell a strike from a ball, a fast ball from a curve. Your batting average is dynamite with some help from your eyes.

Eyes. Fingers. Height. Or your long legs for high jumping at a track meet. Or your wide shoulders for the free-style stroke at a swimming meet. Sure—you're proud of your body. You've got something going for you in sports, some things you've inherited from your parents.

And after listing your favorite parts you're ready to face certain things you don't like about your body. For example, maybe you're the slowest boy on your soccer team. Or in an ice-hockey game you can't keep up with the other skaters because you fall down too often. So you hate your legs. In gymnastics you can't even do a handstand, never mind a somersault. You complain that your body won't balance. After that you complain about your hands. You compare your slow punch to a boxer's punch on TV. He's got the quick hands. Yours couldn't connect with a parked bus they're so slow.

Strength Is the Answer

I train with athletes your age every week. When we first start working with weights

1

Strengthen your body
and you will improve in
every sport you play.

together, I ask each boy just exactly what he wants to improve about himself. These are the answers I hear over and over. I want to:

• pass the football forty yards instead of twenty.
• jump high enough to slamdunk.
• hit homers.
• steal more bases.
• kick more goals.
• swim farther.
• ski without falling down.
• play better.
• win!

From this list of answers you might decide that the boys are all asking for something different. You might guess they've made me a long Christmas gift list, and I'm supposed to be Santa. They want (1) power (2) speed (3) quickness (4) agility (5) coordination and (6) balance in order to be better athletes.

True, these are the basic athletic abilities. They're what you need to do well in any sport, from football to Frisbee. These abilities separate winners from losers. Think for yourself what happens if you increase your shoulder *power*. That's right!

You would throw, pass, and even toss a ball farther. More leg power would help you jump higher for slamdunking. If you're both *quick* and *fast*, your chances of stealing bases are better. Greater *agility* sharpens your kick in a soccer match. Better *coordination* and *balance* will keep you upright on ice skates or on a skateboard.

No doubt about it: Improving these abilities will improve your scores.

But if you're strong, every gift on your Christmas athletic list will arrive without Santa. In working to increase your muscle *strength* you are also automatically improving your quickness, speed, agility, coordination, balance, and power (speed plus strength). Improved muscular fitness will also lengthen your endurance and promote greater flexibility.

All of these benefits from lifting weights! For weight training is the best way to build strength. I'm going to show you how to train.

Your Muscles

Muscles are your body's main support. You have more than 600 muscles, and these make up nearly 50 percent of your body's total weight. Your muscles produce movement in every part of your body. They *bend* your arm at the elbow when you hug a football on a touchdown run. They *straighten* your arm to spike the football in the endzone. Muscles *turn* your palms up to catch a pass, turn your palms down to push a tackler. Muscles *raise* your leg to make a kickoff. They *hold* your body in a squat for a goal-line stand.

Pulling. Pushing. Gripping. Lifting. Muscles are exerting *force*. Your strength is the amount of force that your muscles are capable of exerting.

Muscles grow and become stronger when they work against resistance. Suppose, for example, that each morning you had to carry wood for a fire. After that, suppose you worked all day as a bricklayer's helper: unloading cement from a truck; hauling bricks up ladders; mixing cement by hand.

After work you spend an hour digging in your vegetable garden. By bedtime you might be tired, but you'd be strong. That's because your muscles have been working against resistance week after week.

Not many American boys work their muscles in these ways any more. Instead, they spend much of their time in a classroom sitting still. And they sit in front of TV sets and in Superdomes, where they watch sports in comfort while their muscles stay inactive. The few hours each week that most boys spend playing sports are not enough to make a big difference in strength. Athletes ride to school and then wonder why their legs get tired in a soccer game. They carry nothing heavier than a few books around all week and then wonder why they can't carry a backpack on weekends.

In general, the muscles of American boys today are underdeveloped.

I see this every week in my gym. The beginning boys are unable to lower themselves on the dip bars. They can't chin themselves, either. They jump rope for less than a minute and quit with tired legs. I'm always sorry to see them slouched on a bench after a few pushups and situps. I know they aren't the top athletes on their teams, because in any sport you can name, the good *strong* players will beat the good weak players.

"It's time to muscle up," I tell my beginners as they pick up their dumbbells to train with me. Then I explain about lifting weights.

Working with Weights

Your muscles must be *overloaded* in order for their strength to increase. Muscles grow when they are forced to put out more energy. If you demand more from them they will adapt to the stress by becoming stronger.

Weights demand more from your muscles. And more. And more. That's why lifting them is the best single way to increase your strength. You start by lifting light

Strength is the amount of force that muscles are capable of exerting.

Your muscles must be overloaded to increase strength.

dumbbells for ten times each exercise. When this gets much too easy (because your muscles are growing), you lift your dumbbells twenty times each exercise. Too easy again in a few months, and you lift thirty times each exercise.

Soon you notice how light your dumbbells feel. You add some new exercises with a barbell and with heavier dumbbells. Then your muscles catch up again. You add, they strengthen. Once again you add weight and numbers and new exercises and . . .

Overload your muscles and they will grow. This is one of the two scientific principles behind all my training programs in this book. The other principle is *isolation*, which means you can choose the muscles you want to strengthen. You can isolate them—make them stand out from the crowd of your 600 muscles.

Let's choose a muscle as an example. Squeeze your fingers together into a tight fist. Now bend your forearms at the elbow. Squeeze and bend until your bicep muscle tightens and stands up in the top of your arm. The bicep is one of the main muscles you use in wrestling. It helps you with headlocks and takedowns. Obviously, if you wanted to improve as a wrestler, you'd strengthen your biceps.

Now glance at The Muscleman chart on pages 7–8. My muscles are exactly the same as yours, only bigger and stronger. Our muscles each have names. Those names may look strange to you, like words only a doctor uses. Strange or not, they are easy to learn, especially if you give them nicknames. Your pectorals can be *pecs*. Latissimus dorsi can be *lats*. Deltoids can be *delts*.

As you come to know your main muscle groups you begin to put the muscles together with your sports. Sooner or later you'll decide for yourself just which muscles you want to strengthen. You'll isolate and overload.

Look again at The Muscleman and see yourself.

Locker Room Myths about Weight Training

You've probably heard some discouraging stories about lifting weights. In the locker room a teammate might have told you that strong muscles make you *musclebound* so you can't stretch and bend in games. Muscles slow you down, you've heard. They change you into a hulk. You've also been told that muscles turn to puffy fat, and that's how athletes get out of shape.

Your parents might think that weight training will take up too much of your time when you should be doing homework. And that weights are expensive—worse than skis and boots! All those fancy machines to buy! A few mothers I've talked to even believe that lifting weights will make their boys so hungry they'll be eating all the time. Mothers also worry that lifting weights is dangerous.

There is no truth in these beliefs.

The truth is that your flexibility (bending and stretching moves) will be improved by lifting weights properly. You will not become "tight." Your speed will increase in every sport because strength *is* speed. And

of course, muscles can't turn to fat. Muscle cells and fat cells cannot mix; they are completely different things. Exercising with weights burns fat at the same time muscle cells are being reborn, activated, and stimulated. Vigorous exercise like weight training also tends to reduce appetite, not increase it, as many mothers have long believed.

In only two hours a week—less time than you spend watching a football game on TV—you can train on any one of the programs in this book. Your beginning equipment costs about the same as a baseball bat. Your intermediate-program equipment costs less than a catcher's mitt and mask. Weight training is safer than baseball, basketball, football—safer than any contact sport.

So next time the lifting myths start flying around your locker room or dinner table, say "Roger Staubach." That great quarterback trains with weights all winter and spring between football seasons. Has Staubach's program made him slow or fat or musclebound? Or say "Olympic swimmers." The American winners train with weights and still have time to swim six hours a day before and after school.

Or say "Franco Columbu." For a long time now I have been the world's strongest bodybuilder, and I started training with a pair of second-hand dumbbells.

Young Athletes and Weights

Another myth you may often hear is that weights are for men, not for boys. You've been told that boys have underdeveloped bodies, which need to grow "naturally," without being pushed into adult methods of exercise. You've never seen a book about "muscleboys." You've probably never seen their pictures. So you and your parents might be puzzled and even startled by my programs for young athletes.

My programs are among the first of what eventually will be dozens by many writers. This is because research in America and in European countries has proved the impor-

The Muscleman (front)

A1: Biceps
A3: Radial flexor
A4: Forearm
A6: Long palmar tendon
A7: Triceps
C1: Pectoralis major (pectorals)
C3: Deltoids

D1: Rectus abdominus
D4: Abdominus oblique
E1: Latissimus dorsi
E2: Trapezius
F1: Quadriceps
G1: Gastrocnemius
G2: Anterior tibialis
G5: Soleus

The Muscleman (back)

A1: Brachio radials
A2: Short radial extensor
A3: Biceps
A5: Triceps lateral head
A6: Triceps long head
B1, B2, B3: Deltoids
C1: Trapezius
C3: Lattissimus dorsi
C6: Rhomboideus
C7: Erector spinae
C8: External obliques
C10: Gluteus maximus
D2: Biceps femoris
D4: Gastrocnemius
D5: Soleus
D6: Achilles tendon

When I talk to parents about weight training I argue against the lifting myths.

tant advantages of weight lifting for youngsters. And the same research disproves old-fashioned beliefs about the supposed harm to young muscles, tendons, and joints.

Training with weights has become a fact of life in Eastern European countries that have vigorous Olympic sports programs. In America, weight training for gymnastics, swimming, diving, skating, and running is common for athletes—boys *and* girls—nine years old and over. For them, weights build usable strength safely. Further, a U.S.A. Junior Olympic lifting program reaches boys of all sizes and weights. Pee wee meets

bring together seven-year-olds to compete against each other in the snatch and in the clean and jerk. Their competition is based on research findings that show lifting to be safe because, among other reasons, it promotes harmonious development of the whole muscular system.

I am not suggesting that all boys of every young age should be forced to lift heavy weights for long hours just so they can win every Saturday in their league games.

Far from it. I have written down the very programs I use (and have been using for years) with boys ages 9–14. These are moderate lifting schedules based on muscle research. They take beginners through a series of simple dumbbell exercises chosen to develop their general muscle groups before training specific muscles for certain sports. Boys nine and over can safely graduate to the intermediate program. They will find it challenging without being too stressful and taxing. The advanced programs can be safely followed by boys 12–14 who complete their intermediate programs.

My young friend Chris will show you each exercise. He trains with me regularly. And now we would both like to train with you.

2

Growing Up and Filling Out: Franco in Photos

The day Chris began training with me I showed him my scrapbook. He wanted to know what I looked like when I was "little."

I grew up in Italy, where cameras aren't as inexpensive and plentiful as they are in the United States. Because my parents couldn't afford a camera I have no photographs of myself as a young boy. The pictures I do have in my scrapbook begin when I became a boxer. The earliest ones do make me look "little" compared to my muscular development in later years, after I'd been training with weights.

I showed Chris my scrapbook because I wanted him to see what a set of weights and the habit of lifting them can do for a human body. Certainly you don't need muscles like mine to be an outstanding athlete. But by following my own progress you can get a sense of what is possible to achieve with your own body. Then you can decide how far you want to go for your sport.

At my job. Notice my narrow forearms. Watch them grow in the next seven photographs.

1966
Here I am on the German powerlifting team.

1968
Now I'm Mr. Italy.

1969
Then Mr. Europe.

1970
More muscles and a new title—Mr. Universe.

1971   The same muscles for a new title—Mr. International.

1976
Mr. Olympia! Lots of hard work with the weights in those five missing years.

Below, Mr. Movie Star. Muscles win games and also starring roles in movies.

3

Before You Start Lifting

Before you start lifting you have to make six important decisions. I say "important" because each of them will deeply affect your future training. You'll stay with weight lifting or quit in disappointment according to your decisions.

Where you lift must not be a matter of chance. You should choose a place that is quiet, a place large enough for you to move freely with your weights. You need about eight feet of headroom. If you have a bedroom alone this can make a home gym, provided there is space enough. If you share a bedroom with a brother (or brothers), you may find it difficult to get the quiet you need for lifting, unless your brother trains along with you—seriously trains.

There is nothing worse for your training than being interrupted or heckled. Losing concentration can cause you to quit for the day before you've finished your routine. Quitting early one day lures you to quit

early again and again. For this reason you're better off in the basement of your family's house even if you're in the furnace room or laundry room. A basement gym is a vast improvement over a room upstairs, where everyone comes and goes, the phone rings, and the TV blares. Better still is the garage. If the family car can be parked outside while you train you'll have all the space you need. And in privacy you'll be able to count your lifts, write the number down, and concentrate on your movements.

After you've chosen a place to train, think of it and speak of it as your gym. Your gym will help set the mood for each session. Little by little it can be equipped with official training gear: an adjustable bench; dip bars; a chinning bar; a mirror; and of course your own weights.

What you lift makes an enormous difference in your attitude toward weight training. To save money some boys start on their

Unlike other sports equipment, dumbbells never wear out.

first program by lifting a brick in each hand. Or a plastic bottle full of water. Or a jar of pickles! This is nonsense. It's like playing catcher with your hand wrapped in a beach towel. You get no feeling for the baseball or for the sport.

Once you decide that weight training will help you become a better athlete you should buy two dumbbells, five pounds each. Together they cost less than $5.00. They and your beginning program and gym are all you need for six months of training. Now lifting becomes *professional*. Your fingers warm the dumbbells. They feel real, not like cement, plastic, or glass in your hands. You have the urge to keep lifting after you commit yourself to official equipment.

Dumbbells can be found in almost any sports store and at large department stores like Sears and Penneys. Dumbbells also come in sets with a barbell. These are starter sets and include 110 pounds of assorted weights (called *plates*) along with bars, screws, collars, and sleeves. Some stores will deliver weights. When they arrive at

your gym you simply read the directions and fit your dumbbells and barbell together. (See drawing.) The best thing about weight sets is that you can change the plates on the bars, adding weight as you become stronger in months ahead.

The next best thing is that unlike much sports equipment—footballs, basketballs, baseballs, for example—weights never wear out.

Learn *how to grip* your weights correctly, for a weak or incorrect grip causes many problems, including uncomfortable body positions while lifting, dropping weights that ruin floors, loss of peak lifting power, and injuries.

These are two grips that you'll need to know for all the training programs in the coming chapters:

1. **UNDERGRIP.** Your fingers encircle the bar from beneath with your palms up and your thumbs encircling the bar from above. (See picture.) The under-grip is used mainly in exercises for the

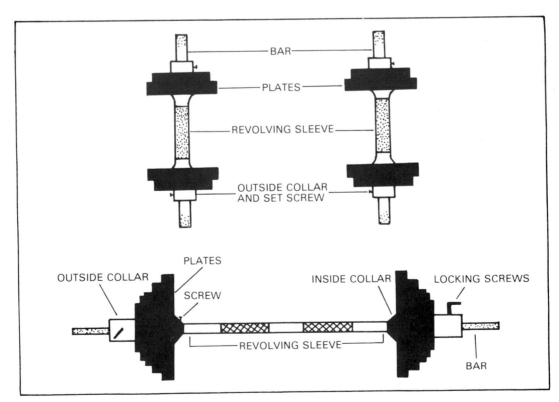

Dumbbells (the kind you assemble) and barbell.

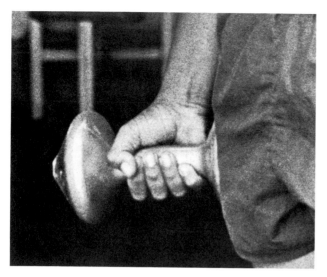

Undergrip

Overgrip

biceps. It's not used to lift a weight overhead.

2. **OVERGRIP.** This is used in all overhead lifts. Your fingers encircle the bar from above with palms down toward the floor. Your thumbs encircle the bar from beneath. (See picture.)

A sound grip develops stronger hands and forearms, tightens ligaments, places nerves under control, and gives you security while lifting. A good gripper is a strong lifter.

The time of day *when you lift* will also affect your training. For me, a workout is a magic hour. It's part of my day when everything goes right. I look forward to that moment when I'll pick up my first dumbbell to begin.

Because of this importance I have a regular hour for workouts. I stick to a schedule. I never try to cram a workout into my time for seeing patients or into my busy social evenings. Instead I organize all my duties around my afternoon hour in the gym.

Weight-training coaches disagree on a perfect time of day for lifting, but I believe that afternoons are best, especially the hours between 2:30 and 5:30. By then your body is warmed up and working well. Your mind is clear because your classes are over.

Your homework can wait until after dinner. The only conflicts you might have are a long sports practice or jobs to do for the family or maybe a music lesson.

I realize that some of you will be unable to train in the afternoon hours and that you'll have to choose another time. As you choose, consider these guidelines:

1. Train at the same hour each time.

2. Don't jump out of bed in the morning and start lifting. Warm up first. If this is your only time to train, be sure to do more warm-up exercises than the few I mention in the beginning program.

3. Try to finish training an hour before eating. Try to begin training at least an hour after eating. If you train on top of a meal you'll feel sluggish.

4. Try never to miss a workout. By staying on schedule you build up a rhythm that is good for your mind as well as for your body.

Another decision that influences both your mind and body is *what you wear* to a workout. If you're in a dirty ragged sweatshirt and old baggy sweatpants you'll feel like a slouch who's playing a very minor sport. "What am I doing down here in the basement?" you might ask as you catch a look at your grubby self. Wearing your league baseball or soccer uniform wouldn't be right, either. And school clothes would

Wearing a "uniform" will give you a lift.

be too tight for the movements of weight training.

Let's face it—clothes are an important ingredient of sports. The right uniform can make you feel and play like a pro when you take your position in a game. The same is true of weight training: A special uniform will give you a lift while lifting.

You don't need to buy something new. From your summer clothes choose a pair of shorts and a tank top that are loose fitting but not sloppy. In this brief uniform you'll be able to watch your muscles as you exercise. On cold days, if you're training in a garage gym, it's best to have your muscles covered in a sweatsuit. Keeping muscles warmed up helps you progress quickly through your day's programs and also prevents injuries.

I've saved your most crucial decision until last. Now you must think about *why* you are starting a weight-training program. The answers you give will become *your goals*.

Goals help you stick to a program. Without them you are tempted either to skip a workout altogether or train half-heartedly if you're tired, upset, or if you're in a pinch for time. On those days when you have a "perfect" excuse to avoid the challenge and discipline of a workout, remember your goals.

Your long-range goal is to become a better athlete by increasing your strength. Always keep strength in mind as you head toward your gym. You should also decide on more personal long-range goals. For example, decide that you will weight train in order to be chosen for a league soccer team. More than that you want to play first string. Or decide you want to win your team's most valuable player award if you already play first string.

Write down your long-range goals, and keep them on a wall of your gym. Here's a sample list for an all-around athlete. These goals may give you ideas of your own.

- **To allow fewer goals than last year to be scored by opposing players (if you're a soccer goalie)**

- **To come through basketball season without injury**
- **To improve batting average by 25 points**
- **To run 100 yards 5 seconds faster than last season**
- **To be chosen team captain on the basis of outstanding play**

Don't set your long-range goals too high or too low. And once set, concentrate on them as you change into your lifting uniform. Then, warming up, concentrate on your daily goals:

- **To complete all exercises in the program**
- **To do them correctly, according to the photographs and instructions**
- **To try for a slightly faster progression from exercise to exercise (rest less between lifts)**

Monthly goals are the hardest to set, but these you need most of all. Accomplishing them will psych you up for the next month of training. One good way of setting monthly goals is to depend on a tape measure. Before you lift your very first dumbbell, ask your dad or mom to measure your upper arms, forearms, chest, thighs, and calves. Measure them again each month and write down your progress. A gain of only $\frac{1}{16}$ of an inch on arms, forearms, etc., is real progress for a month.

Another way to set monthly goals is to pay attention to what others say about you. After you've been training with weights for a month you'll probably be told by your sports coach that you're playing your position better. He'll mention also that you have more stamina. Your dad will tell you that you seem to have more energy, that you look healthier. Your mom will notice that you stand up straighter and don't get grumpy as often.

These comments can be turned into monthly goals:

- **To score two more goals (or touchdowns or runs) per month**

- To play a complete basketball (or soccer) game without resting once on the bench
- To swim 25 more laps of the pool per month
- To improve as a team leader by taking a share of blame for a loss (It takes strength of character to lose gracefully. Training with weights can strengthen character as well as muscles.)

Many athletes begin weight training without a single goal. Before long they drop out of their home gyms. You can psych yourself up to continue lifting by setting and meeting goals.

Why will you train with weights? Where and when and what will you lift. How will you grip, and what will you wear? Ask your mother and father and coach to help you decide. Then turn the page and start lifting.

4

Beginning to Lift:
A First Training Program
for Young Athletes

Today is the day to pick up your weights and begin.

But before you turn the page to your first exercise, the squat, you must make sure you're warmed up and ready to lift an extra ten pounds. The dumbbells will feel lighter, and your whole body will feel fresher and more flexible if you get your blood circulating faster right now.

Jumping rope is an excellent way to warm up. Running in place or going for a short run around the block will warm you up fast. Stretching in all four directions will limber your legs and spine. For example, stand with your feet about two feet apart and with your arms stretched above your head. Stretch up as far as you can. Then bend at your waist. Touch the floor with your fingertips while keeping your legs straight. Repeat this ten times. As you are stretching upward, pretend you're try-

ing to reach the ceiling. This extra effort will make your face flush.

A pink face and a damp forehead are good signs that you're warmed up and ready to lift.

Quick Warm-Up Schedule

Jump rope for ½ minute or until you count to 30 while jumping.

or

Run in place for ½ minute.

then

Stretch up and down 10 times.

Here is another quick warm-up schedule: When you have learned the first eight exercises of the beginning program, you can do these *without the weights* as a way of warming up. Do them each three times, then take

Dumbbell squat (1)

a half-minute break before starting your squats with the dumbbells.

The dumbbells that Chris is using weigh five pounds each. You will be using this weight for the entire beginning program. Chris and I do these exercises three times a week: Monday, Wednesday, and Friday. You may choose to lift on Tuesday, Thursday, and Saturday instead. Just make sure you have a full day of rest after each day of training.

As you train remember these tips:

1. Take at least 2 seconds to raise your weights. *Don't throw them up.* Raising weights slowly will cause you to work harder.
2. Lowering weights is easier than raising them, so you will mistakenly want to drop the weights fast instead of slowly lowering them. To remind yourself not to drop the dumbbells, count to 4 as you lower. Think "Smooth, smooth, smooth, smooth" 4 times.

And now, begin with Exercise 1.

Exercise 1: Dumbbell Squat

Stand up straight, holding the dumbbells at your side. Squat down to the position Chris is in. Then up, then down again. Go down until your thighs are level with your knees.

Look straight ahead when doing this exercise.

The squat will strengthen your thighs and buttocks. It also helps to expand your rib cage so that your heart and lungs have more room to grow.

First month: Do 1 set of 20 squats

Second and third months: Do 2 sets of 20 squats

Fourth, fifth, and sixth months: Do 3 sets of 20 squats

Rest a minute and go on to Exercise 2.

Exercise 2: Standing Dumbbell Press

Hold the dumbbells at shoulder level, the same way Chris holds them in position 2A. Press them above your head to position 2B.

Lower slowly and press again. Keep your back straight.

You are strengthening your shoulders and upper arms.

First month: Do 1 set of 15

Second and third months: Do 2 sets of 15

Fourth, fifth, and sixth months: Do 3 sets of 15

Exercise 3: Lunges with Dumbbells

This exercise builds muscles in your

Standing dumbbell press (2A)   (2B)

Lunge with dumbbells (3)

thighs and buttocks and will help make your lower body more flexible.

Stand up straight with a dumbbell in each hand. Step forward as far as you can on your left foot. As you step forward, lower yourself to the position Chris takes in picture 3. Notice that his right knee almost touches the floor. Raise up, then stand up straight again. Put your right foot forward and lunge again.

Hold your head and upper body straight during this exercise.

First month: 1 set of 20
Second and third months: 2 sets of 20
Fourth, fifth, and sixth months: 3 sets of 20

Exercise 4: Standing Lateral Raises

In football, a lateral is a pass thrown to the side. In picture 4, lateral raises, you will lift your dumbbells to the side. Raise the dumbbells slightly higher than shoulder level. Lower them slowly. Raise. Lower.

Standing lateral raises (4A)

(4B)

This is one of the most important exercises for your shoulder muscles. Your neck muscles are also working hard. You can feel how hard yourself in this simple experiment: lay your left hand against the right side of your neck as you raise your right arm. You should be able to feel your neck muscles popping up under your hand.

First month: *Raise each arm* 20 times
Second and third months: 2 sets of 20
Fourth, fifth, and sixth months: 3 sets of 20

Exercise 5: Standing Front Raises

With a 5-pound dumbbell in each hand, raise your arms one at a time to the height

Standing front raises (5)

Bent-over one-arm rowing (6A)   (6B), below

Standing triceps press (7A)

(7B)

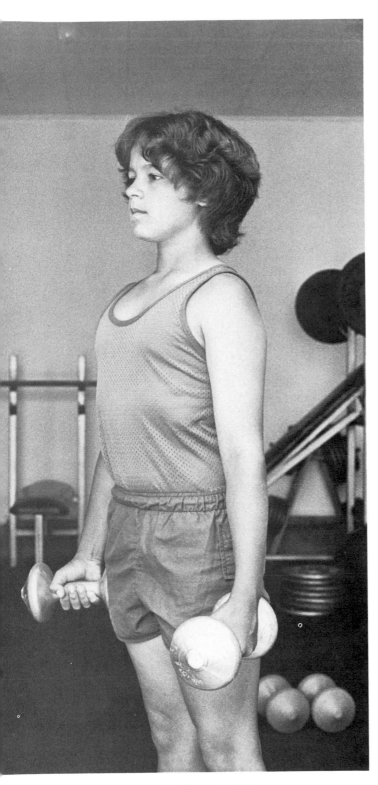 

Standing dumbbell curl (8A)   (8B)

Chris is holding his right arm. Raise and lower in a slow rhythm.

You are strengthening your shoulders and upper arms as you do this exercise.

First month: *Raise each arm* 20 times
Second and third months: 2 sets of 20
Fourth, fifth, and sixth months: 3 sets of 20

Exercise 6: Bent-over One-arm Rowing

Look at the picture of Chris (6A). Place your right hand on a bench or on another support like a sturdy table or chair. Spread your feet in his same position. Pull the dumbbell to the height of 6B. Lower and pull again. Breathe in as you pull up. Change hands and repeat the set of 20.

Only your arms and shoulders should move during this exercise.

First month: 1 set of 20
Second and third months: 2 sets of 20
Fourth, fifth, and sixth months: 3 sets of 20

Exercise 7: Standing Triceps Press

Stand comfortably. Picture 7A shows the starting position, elbow up and bent. While keeping the elbow up, straighten the arm to position 7B. Repeat 15 times, then change the dumbbell to your other hand and repeat 15 times.

The triceps is the muscle directly under Chris's left hand. As you press your dumbbell you will feel the triceps working.

First month: 2 sets of 15 each arm
Second and third months: 3 sets of 15 each arm
Fourth, fifth, and sixth months: 4 sets of 15 each arm

Exercise 8: Standing Dumbbell Curl

Stand comfortably holding a dumbbell in

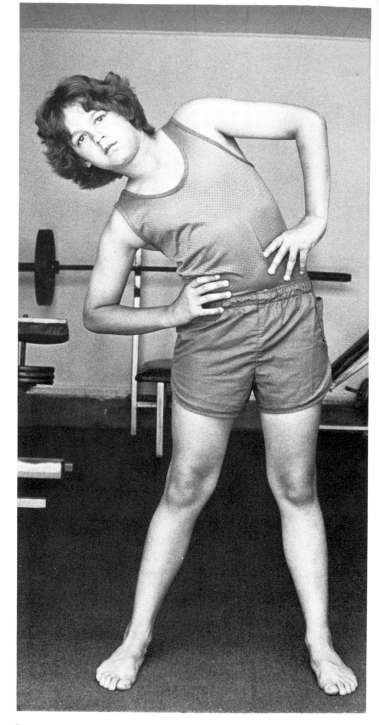

Standing side bends (9)

each hand. Notice that your palms should be facing your body (8A). As you lift the dumbbells, turn your palms as shown in 8B. Curl to a height of about 6 inches beyond Chris's arms in 8B.

Your biceps are large muscles in the top fronts of your arms. You will feel them

Standing front leg raises (10)

working as you curl. The biceps and triceps are called *antagonist* muscles. They are paired for movement in the upper arm.

First month: 2 sets of 15
Second and third months: 3 sets of 15
Fourth, fifth, and sixth months: 4 sets of 15

Exercise 9: Standing Side Bends

This exercise will increase your flexibility and strengthen your hips.

Begin by standing up straight. Put your hands on your hips and spread your feet wide. Bend right to left for a total of 20 repetitions.

First month: 2 sets of 20
Second and third months: 2 sets of 30
Fourth, fifth, and sixth months: 3 sets of 30

Exercise 10: Standing Front Leg Raises

Stand with your legs a few inches apart. Hold your arms as Chris holds his. Now raise your right leg to touch your left hand. Lower your leg and raise your left leg to touch your right hand. Continue, alternating legs.

Your hips, abdomen, and thighs are getting a good workout.

First month: 2 sets of 20
Second and third months: 3 sets of 30
Fourth, fifth, and sixth months: 4 sets of 30

5

Talking with Franco

During my years of working with young athletes I have been asked hundreds of times about my training "secrets":

- "Franco, have you made up a secret lift for your arms that no one else knows?"
- "Do you eat food the other guys don't eat? What's your recipe?"
- "Does your doctor prescribe a vitamin that he saves just for you?"
- "You must know some terrific schedules for lifting weights that you never write about in all your books. Tell me and I won't tell."
- "I'll bet you've invented an exercise machine better than the ones other athletes train on!"
- "Franco, explain how many pounds you really lift when you're home alone in your gym."

My answer to these—and to all other questions like them—is always the same: I have no magic weights or food or vitamins. I don't use secret training schedules or hidden machines to build my body into world-class condition. So I can't write a chapter here called "The Secrets That Made Me Mr. Olympia." There are no secrets.

But, of course, I have answers for the many questions that lifters ask me when we're training together. By the time you have gone through the beginning program for several weeks you may be asking these same questions yourself. I hope my answers below will help improve your workouts.

Q. Franco, I told some kids in my school that I was lifting weights at home. One boy bragged about his dad's health club. He said his dad works out on machines that are better than my weights. Do you think *I should be training on those machines?*

Everywhere I travel, young lifters ask for my training "secrets."

A. I want you to look at this picture of Chris training with me in my home gym. Do you see any fancy machines? You do see a long row of dumbbells, the same piece of equipment you're using in the beginning programs. Also you see benches and barbells you'll soon be using in the intermediate and advanced programs.

On the wall above the dumbbells are my dip bars. These cost me less than $20.00 and they aren't machines. The jump ropes are for warming-up exercises. The rug makes our situps more comfortable than a bare cement floor in this garage.

I built this gym in the garage behind my house in Los Angeles, California. The only machine I installed is just behind Chris: a leg-extension machine. You will see me using it much later in the sports program.

I trained on the simple basic equipment in my home gym for the 1976 Mr. Olympia contest. And I won. Now you decide if you need to join a health club with expensive machines.

Q. Some other kids want to come over and lift with me at home, a bunch of them. They say they can help me. Should I be *training with other people around?*

A. Let me tell you from my own experience some of the bad things that can happen when boys get together to train.

You can start gazing around at what the other boys are doing. If they're lifting heavier weights, you might think you have to keep up with them instead of staying on your own program. Heavier weights can lead you to strains and other injuries. If the boys are chatting and gossiping, you will have the impulse to join in. You'll waste

My gym behind my house.

time fooling around between sets, maybe flipping towels and chasing each other. You'll quit early because they do. You might not pick up your weights at all next time if your friends don't show up at your house.

All of this means that you have lost concentration, and concentration is vital for a good workout.

Now for the good news: Training with a partner can help you stick to your program.

As you do your set of squats, your partner can make sure your feet are placed correctly and that you're looking straight ahead. He can count your repetitions along with you. He becomes your own personal cheerleader with "Way-to-go!" as you finish each set. Then you cheer him through his set of lunges. If he gets tired on lunge number 6, you egg him on with "Just 4 more . . . just 3 more." You give him a pat on the back for finishing his workout. You help each other keep going.

With two sets of dumbbells, you can lift together. Facing each other you'll watch for progress in moving smoothly through the beginning program. During the intermediate and advanced programs you can help each other position the barbell for squats, bench presses, and other exercises.

So far, so good. The one problem that you may have with this super partner is if he sometimes doesn't come over to train. Then you're tempted to skip your own workout. If he fails to come three times in a row you've missed a whole week of training. That could cause you to feel like quitting for good.

Never wait for your partner. Go ahead and train alone. Pat yourself on the back when you've finished your last set of the day.

Q. *Why am I so stiff and sore* after my first week of training?

A. I understand how you feel because I've felt that way myself when I start training again after a layoff.

For me, the layoff means I've neglected my muscles. For you, weight training is a new sport, and you're working certain muscles you haven't worked hard before. For both of us, our bodies haven't been flushing toxins (poisons) from our muscles. Those toxins cause soreness. Also our joints are stiff because lubricating fluid has not been moving through them efficiently.

Don't dread the pain of stiffness and soreness. Welcome it as a sign that your muscles are working hard and that your joints are improving in flexibility.

When you add weight or repetitions to your training program your muscles will be working even harder. This causes temporary soreness until your muscles adjust to the demand. Also when you add new exercises to your program you should expect some soreness because a different group of muscles will be working.

Some weight lifters I know have this motto hanging in their gyms: PAIN IS GAIN. Pain shows them that their muscles have been put through a tough workout. I don't recommend such workouts for your regular schedule. But when you increase your training load every few months, you'll feel the pain (stiffness, soreness) in gain.

Q. Can I *skip around in the order of exercises?*

A. No! For sure, some exercises will be easier than others, and you'll want to do them first or maybe save the easiest for last as a treat. There will be days when you'll want to skip your hardest exercises completely.

The *order* of exercises is as important to your progress as the *kind of exercise*, the *number* of repetitions, and the *pounds* of weight. Train your body in the Columbu schedule, not in some goofy order that you make up from day to day as your favorite lifts change.

Soon your hard exercises will become easier, and your easy exercises will become almost effortless.

Q. My eyes wander all over the room when I'm lifting, Franco. *Where should I be looking?*

A. Every part of your body has a specific position in weight lifting. Glance back at the pictures of Chris in your beginning program, and notice how carefully he positions his feet, his arms, and even his eyes.

Your eyes have only two positions: looking at the weight or looking straight ahead.

First you look at the weight to see if you're holding it correctly. You check your grip. You notice how far apart your hands are spaced on the barbell. Then you look straight ahead because this will help your balance while you exercise.

You won't get bored looking straight ahead if you have a mirror on that wall. You can watch your muscles work. You become more aware of your body's strength if you watch yourself progress through every program.

Q. I never know *how to breathe when I'm lifting.* Everyone I ask says something different. Would you explain once and for all.

A. You're right to ask about breathing. No detail is too small to overlook when you're really interested in improving.

Here are five rules that I follow:

1. Never hold your breath while training. You can get dizzy if you do, or you can even pass out.
2. Breathe deeply. Deep breathing improves your circulation. This means more oxygen gets to the muscles being exercised. Muscles work harder with more oxygen.
3. Breathe in through your nose, out through your mouth.
4. As you begin each exercise, take a deep breath. Then, at the point that the exer-

Looking straight ahead will help you keep balance while lifting.

cise makes its greatest demand on your body, let your breath out. In other words, *inhale* when you're beginning, *exhale* when you're pushing or pulling or pressing or lifting, etc.

5. If you are training inside (in your room or in the garage, for example), take a break about halfway through your workout. Go outside and breathe fresh air. This pause will give you immediate vigor.

Q. Franco, I always just sit around resting *between exercises. Is there anything special I should be doing?*

A. Your resting period should be as short as possible—no more than one minute between sets. As you progress through the programs you should try to shorten your rests: one-half minute is a good target. Keep a clock in your gym so you won't need to guess.

Avoid temptations to rest longer. Don't sit down. Don't prowl from room to room. Don't go to the kitchen for a snack. Wait until after your workout to eat. Never telephone a friend or watch TV during a workout. You'll ruin your concentration. You'll want to stop lifting and follow the other guy's action. Instead, keep up your own action.

Stay with a routine. As you finish your repetitions of an exercise, write the number 10 next to the exercise in your notebook of workouts. Then breathe deeply, and walk around the room so you don't cool down. A minute will pass in no time. Do your next set of exercises. Write down the number. Step to your mirror and strike a pose to see your muscles. Flex your arms several times. During your next minute of rest, flex your legs. Check them for progress, front and back.

As you watch your body in the mirror you will gain concentration. You'll want to go on lifting, not rest more often.

Between sets, check your progress by posing in front of your gym mirror.

Q. *What's the best thing to do when I'm finished training for the day?* Take a cold shower? A long nap? Or what?

A. Champion weight lifters never head for the locker room without warming down.

After your final exercises, put your weights in a place where no one will stumble over them.

Now it's time to relax. Stand with your feet apart. Shake your arms and hands the way you've seen swimmers shake them to relax at the starting line. Bend over from your waist, and let your body hang as loose as possible. Let your hands hang while you breathe completely out. Raise up and breathe in. Repeat several times.

A warm shower comes next. If you're hungry, eat a fresh fruit instead of a cookie. Drink water instead of a sugary soft drink.

Q. When I started training with weights, two other boys in my apartment building were training with me. They quit already. They said it's boring. To tell you the truth, Franco, *I'm bored, too. Every day the same old exercises!*

A. If you're bored that means you've lost sight of your goals.

Think back to the day when you first started weight training. You set yourself the goal of getting stronger. But like any other improvement in sports, strength doesn't happen overnight. Strength happens over time if you work for it.

So you work. There is no hiding place from lifting. You're either doing it or you're not. Your willpower must take you into your gym three days a week. Your program has strengthened hundreds of young athletes. Think about that as you lift. Think of your goals. Think of your muscles. Already the weights feel lighter, and you feel faster in your sport and quicker.

Don't be a quitter. Of course your exercises are the same all during your beginning programs. That's because they get results—they are winning exercises. Why fool around with losers?

At the moment you want to quit while you're training, squeeze the dumbbell or

It helps to squeeze the barbell for a psych on your last repetition.

barbell harder and keep lifting. Another good psych-up is to ask your mom or dad to take some photographs of you early in the beginning program. Hang these in your gym. Every two or three weeks, pose for some new ones. Side by side the photographs will prove your progress. Study them between sets.

Here's one more psych-up I tell boys who train with me:

Think way ahead to your future. As an outstanding athlete you'll be eligible for prep-school and college scholarships. You'll have a shot at the Olympics. Professional teams will come looking for you. You'll earn lots of money and travel widely. I have been around the world many times, competing on every continent except Antarctica. I am a rich man today because I was not bored with weight training.

Q. Franco, I'm not one bit bored with weight lifting. I like it so much *I'd train every day. Wouldn't I get stronger if I did?*

A. No. You'd get overtrained. You'd lose your zest for working out. You might lose your appetite and not sleep well at night.

Muscles need time to rest between workouts. At your age, muscles need a full day's rest. And you can use the extra time to practice your sport on days you aren't in the gym lifting. You could make up a program

As a world-class athlete, I've competed on six continents.

Training with weights
is a natural high.

to improve your skills of throwing, catching, kicking, heading, running, etc.

Q. Some kids on my team at school say there are pills to make them grow bigger muscles. They say they know other pills to take in the locker room that will help them run faster during games. Franco, *should I be taking these pills?*

A. There are always athletes looking for an easy way to improve, and taking a pill is certainly easier than lifting a dumbbell.

But for any sport you play you can't find a quick and easy solution to your skill and fitness problems. Pills won't build muscles or stamina or endurance; exercise will.

Pills won't improve your skills; practice will. Drugs won't make you run or swim or skate faster, throw more accurately, or hit harder. Nothing you can swallow on the sidelines will cause you to be braver in a game. Mental toughness comes partly from knowing you are physically strong.

Very simply: Drugs fail to help athletes improve.

And that goes for all illegal drugs that you may see older boys using to get "high." Nothing you can smoke or sniff will give you the fantastic feeling of energy and motion that you get from a hard workout in your sport.

Playing sports makes you feel free. Lifting weights is a natural high.

6

The Habit of Training: Intermediate and Advanced Programs for Young Athletes

After six months on the beginning program you're about to graduate!

But before turning the page to your intermediate program, take a short vacation from the gym. You deserve it! Don't even look at your weights for a whole week.

Then come back refreshed. A layoff will keep you from getting *stale*. That's what athletes say when they've trained hard for many months on the same routine. They've lost some of their enthusiasm and are maybe a little overtired. They know it's time for a change. So they take a break. They return to a different program. They sometimes find a new training partner to inspire them.

Your intermediate equipment will give you a mental lift. You'll be using a barbell and a bench. Your bench can be one you already have around the house: a piano bench or maybe a redwood bench that goes

with a picnic table. Or, in a sports shop you can buy an official weight bench for about $30.00. You'll also need a block of wood for your new exercises, barbell squats and calf raises. It should be 2–3 inches high and about a foot long.

To make gains in weight training you must demand more from your muscles. Already in the beginning programs you've discovered two basic ways of working harder:

1. increasing your number of repetitions of each exercise
2. increasing your number of sets

Further, in the programs to follow you'll be

3. adding new exercises
4. increasing the amount of weight you lift:

7½-pound dumbbells for the intermediate exercises and 2½-pound plates on
each end of your barbell

And it's up to you to

5. shorten the time you rest between exercises

Because you'll be working with heavier
weights, safety precautions are even more
important. If you turn through the pictures
in this chapter you'll see me working
closely with Chris. I'm handing him the
barbell in some exercises. I'm standing
near him in case he loses balance. If he does
I'll catch his barbell.

Standing
barbell press (11A)

(11B)

If you don't have a partner for safety you might ask your dad or mom to help you through the first days of intermediate training. Once you get the hang of each exercise, you'll find a rhythm, pace, and balance that allow you to train safely alone. You'll discover your limits of strength and energy. Don't try to push beyond them by taking risks alone with heavier weights and extra repetitions.

As usual, you'll need to warm up before you train. Do a little rope jumping, jogging in place, and a few light exercises that include bending and stretching moves. You may feel stiff and sore for a few weeks on the intermediate program because new muscles are working and old ones are working harder. If you do, take plenty of time to warm up, until you are moving freely and smoothly around your gym.

Then begin with the standing barbell press.

Exercise 11: Standing Barbell Press

Stand straight with your feet about shoulder-width apart. Like Chris, rest the barbell on your chest. Use an overhand grip.

Press the barbell from your chest to the overhead position in 11B. Return to the starting position and repeat.

The quadricep muscle in your legs, the tricep in your arms, and the deltoid in your shoulders are strengthened when you do this exercise.

Your barbell should have a 2½-pound plate at each end.

Six months to a year: Do 2 sets of 15 repetitions

Exercise 12: The Squat

Stand with your heels on a wooden block. Using a wide grip, hold the barbell on your shoulders as in 12A. Lower your body to position 12B. Raise. Lower. Continue.

Look straight ahead to keep from tipping over.

Make certain that your legs bend from the front, not with your knees going further apart. To make sure of this, stand with your toes about 10 to 14 inches apart, but no more.

This is the most important of all thigh exercises. At first it will feel awkward to you, but after a few weeks of training your form will improve.

Six months to a year: Do 2 sets of 15

Exercise 13: Hack Squat

In 13A I am handing Chris the barbell. This makes the hack squat easier for him to begin. You can begin alone by laying the barbell across your bench and picking it up from there.

Use a wooden block under your heels. Holding the barbell behind your legs (13B), squat down, but not so low that the barbell touches the floor (13C). Rise to position 13B again, then squat, rise, continue.

Your thighs—especially your lower thighs—are being strengthened by the hack squat.

Six months to a year: Do 2 sets of 10

Exercise 14: Bench Press

The bench press develops your chest muscles. You will enjoy doing it because of the warmth it brings to your entire upper body.

Lie on the bench. Lift your barbell from the upright hooks or from the hands of your training partner (14A). Or hold it across your legs as you lie down, then move it to position 14B.

Lower the barbell to your chest (14C), keeping the bar level across your chest, not your neck. Inhale as you lower the barbell. Push up and exhale. Repeat.

Six months to a year: Do 3 sets of 10

Exercise 15: Dumbbell Flys

This is another good exercise for your chest.

Lie flat on your bench, a dumbbell in

Squat (12A)

(12B)

each hand. Bend your arms as you lower the dumbbells (15B). Stretch high, returning to the straight-arm starting position (15A).

Six months to a year: Do 2 sets of 15

Exercise 16: Barbell Rowing

Barbell rowing gives your back a good workout, especially your latissimus dorsi muscles.

Stand on the bench holding your barbell in a wide grip. Lean over and let the bar hang to position 16A. Pull it from the hanging position until it touches your abdomen (16B). Lower and repeat. Keep your legs slightly bent.

Hack squat (13A)

(13B)

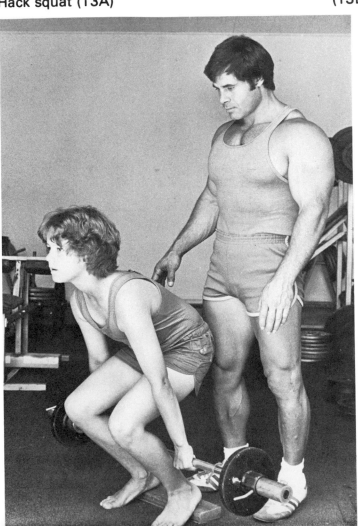

(13C)

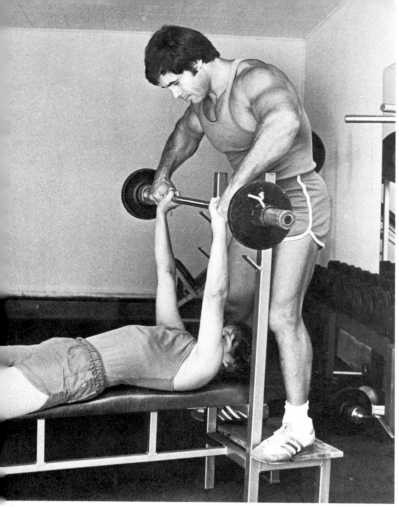

Bench press (partner helping) (14A)

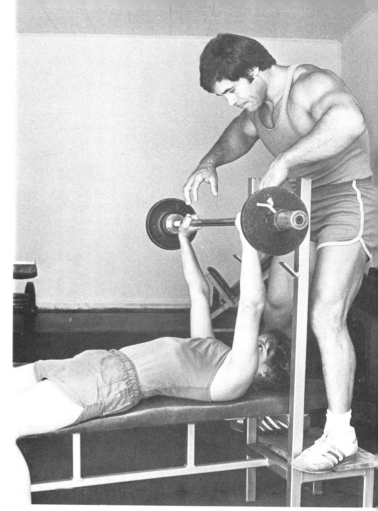

(14B)

(14C)

Flys (15A)

(15B)

Barbell rowing (16A)

(16B)

Bent-over
one-arm rowing (17A)

(17B)

Standing
lateral raises (18)

Standing on the bench lets you lower the barbell further than if you were standing on the floor. The lower the barbell the more you stretch your back muscles.

Six months to a year: Do 2 sets of 10

Exercise 17: Bent-over One-arm Rowing (Same as Exercise 6)

Don't forget to *lower* the dumbbell instead of "dropping" it in a hurry. And pull the dumbbell all the way up until it touches your chest (your pectoralis muscles).

Six months to a year: Do 2 sets of 15 for each arm

Exercise 18: Standing Lateral Raises (Same as Exercise 4)

These strengthen your deltoid muscles.

Notice how Chris looks directly ahead while he raises his dumbbells. This helps him keep his balance and concentration.

Six months to a year: Do 2 sets of 15

Exercise 19: Standing Front Raises (Same as Exercise 5)

Look straight ahead and don't swing the dumbbells. Lift and lower them smoothly. Feel your deltoids working!

Six months to a year: 2 sets of 10

Standing front raises (19)

Exercise 20: Barbell Triceps Press (Seated)

Look at Chris in position 20A. He starts this exercise keeping his elbows tucked in close to his head. He continues by lowering the barbell to position 20B, raising to 20A, then lowering.

His hands are close together but not quite touching each other.

If you train with a partner he should hand you the barbell. If you train alone you can pick up the barbell from the floor and sit down slowly. Then lift it to position 20A.

Six months to a year: 2 sets of 15

58

Barbell
triceps press (seated) (20A)

(20B)

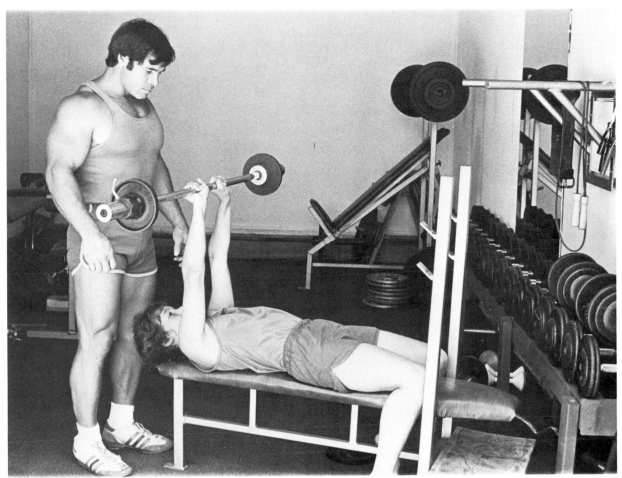

Lying triceps press (21A)

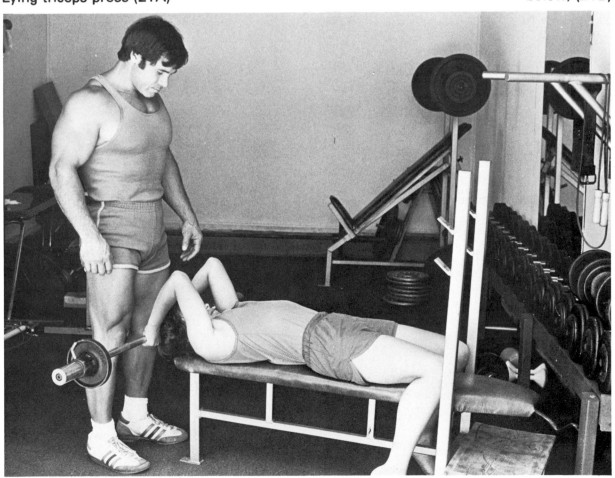

Standing dumbbell curl (22)

Barbell curl (23A)   below, (23B)

Wrist curl (24A)

Exercise 21: Lying Triceps Press

Lie on the bench. Begin the exercise by holding your barbell in position 21A. Notice that Chris has his hands close together. As he lowers the barbell to position 21B his elbows point straight up. He inhales while lowering the weight and exhales when pressing to the starting position.

If you don't have a partner to hand you the barbell, sit down on the bench with the barbell balanced across your thighs. Then lie back and reach for it.

The name of this exercise tells you the main muscle being worked.

Six months to a year: Do 2 sets of 15

Exercise 22: Standing Dumbbell Curl (Same as Exercise 8)

Do not lean backwards when raising the dumbbells. Lower them slowly. You can raise them both at the same time, as Chris does, or alternate raising and lowering your right and left hands.

Six months to a year: Do 2 sets of 15

Exercise 23: Barbell Curl

Use an underhand grip.

Stand erect with the barbell hanging downward across your thighs. Slowly raise the barbell *through* position 23A to the top

(24B)

position (23B). Pause a second at the top, then slowly return the barbell to its starting position and repeat.

Remember not to jerk the barbell, and don't heave with your back. Move smoothly through every position in order to work your biceps.

Six months to a year: Do 2 sets of 12

Exercise 24: Forearm Wrist Curl

Start with your arms supported by a bench or other flat surface. Keep your elbows still and straight, as in 24A. Curl your wrists up to the top position (24B); then allow the dumbbell to roll back down the fingers and return to 24A. Curl up, roll down. Repeat to strengthen your hands and grip.

Six months to a year: Do 2 sets of 15

Exercise 25: Calf Raises

Study the picture of Chris (25).

Stand with your right foot on a block of wood. Bend your nonexercising leg (left leg) at the knee to keep it off the floor. Hold the dumbbell in your right hand. Use your left hand for balance by holding onto the back of a chair or onto a piece of gym equipment.

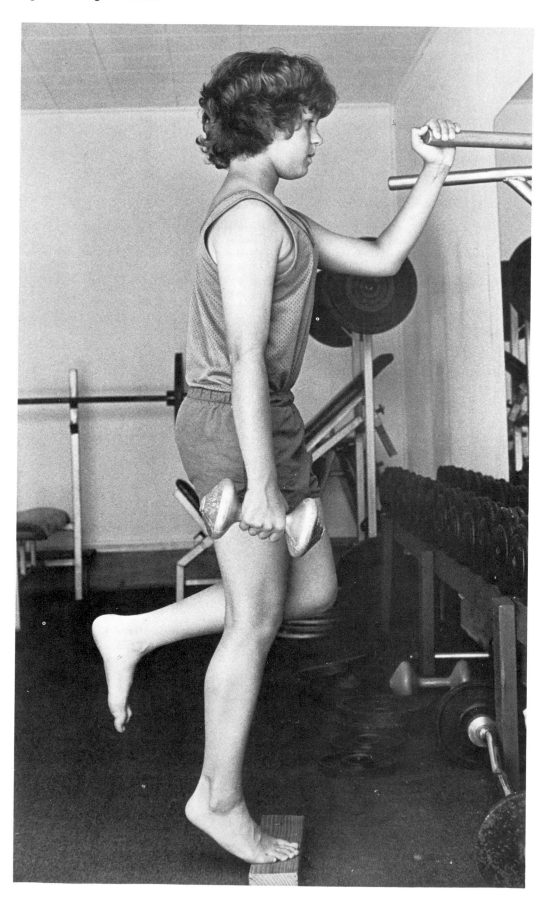

Calf raises (25)

Bench sit-ups (26)

Now begin the exercise: Raise your right heel off the floor while raising up on your toes. Pause. Then lower to the starting position. Raise the heel as high as possible each repetition. The calf muscles in your legs are being worked with this exercise.

Six months to a year: Do 3 sets of 15 repetitions on each leg.

Exercise 26: Bench Situps

You've probably done situps at school in your gym class. Here Chris does a variation by lying on the bench instead of on the floor. All of the different kinds of situps work your abdominal muscles, which support the middle of your body. They help keep you erect and protect your internal organs.

Begin this exercise with your legs straight out and with your head flat on the bench. Raise your head and legs to Chris's position. Then lower yourself to the beginning position. Raise. Lower. Continue.

Six months to a year: Do 2 sets of 20

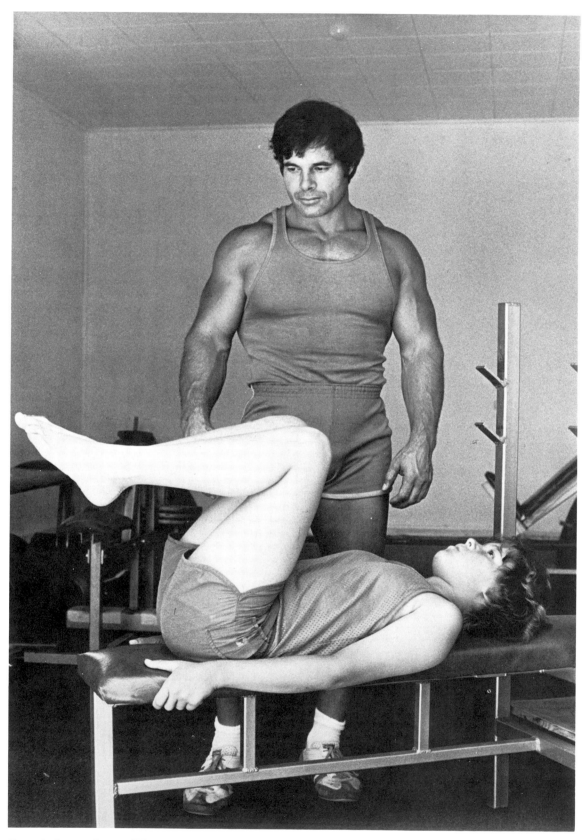

Bench leg raises (27A)

Exercise 27: Bench Leg Raises

Leg raises also work your abdominal muscles. They can be done on the floor some days for a variation.

Lie on the bench in position 27A. Hold on with both hands, and bring your knees to your chest (27B). Then push your legs out straight again.

Six months to a year: Do 2 sets of 20

I have planned the intermediate program so that *you* can decide when you want to "graduate." I have suggested that you stay with the intermediate sets and repetitions for *at least* six months, but *no longer than* a year. In the six-month period you should take several breaks from training so you don't get stale. Relax for a week away from your gym. Then come back and concentrate even harder. Gradually you will feel your body growing used to the intermediate exercises. At the end of six months, if you feel fresh and strong after your workouts you're ready to move on to a new program—the advanced.

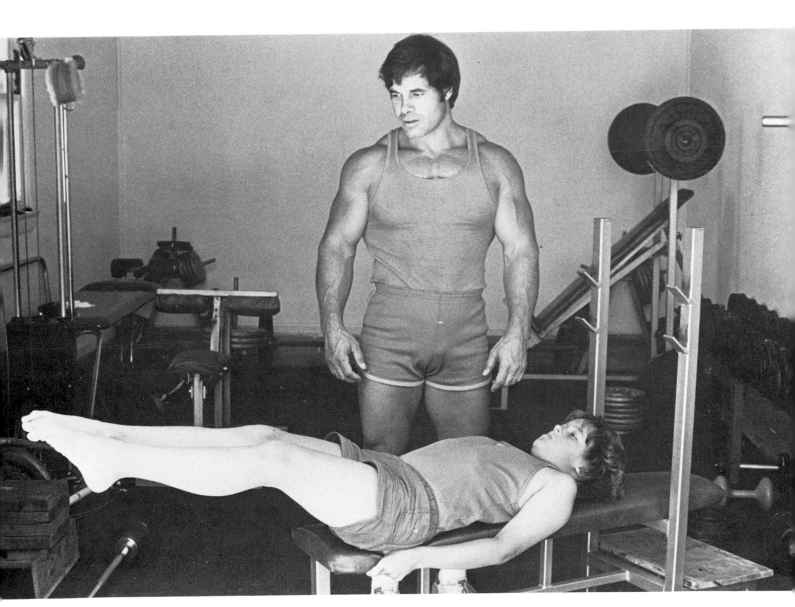

(27B)

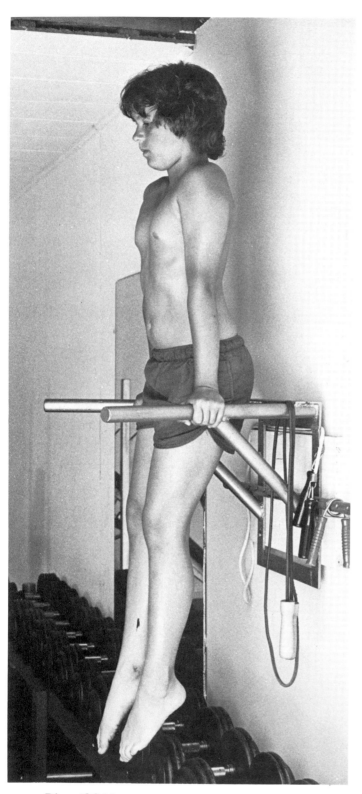

Dips (28A)

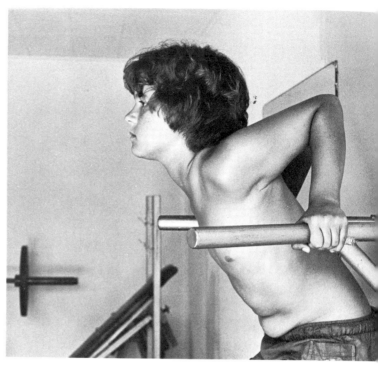

(28B)

Or you may decide to stay with the intermediate program for seven months or eight or nine. If you do, add a new exercise to the end of your schedule: dips. These will give you a real challenge.

Exercise 28: Dips

Bend your arms to lower your body. At first this will be hard. Begin by lowering yourself just a little way. As your strength improves, do one-half the movement. Keep your head and chest forward (28B).

Learning the form and a personal rhythm for dips makes them easier. They work your triceps, deltoids, and pectoralis muscles.

Do 1 set of 5 to begin. Add 1 a week to your set.

Advanced Programs

	1st Year	2nd Year
Standing Barbell Press	3 × 10	4 × 10
Squat	3 × 15	4 × 15
Hack Squat	3 × 10	4 × 10
Bench Press	4 × 10	5 × 10
Dumbbell Flys	3 × 15	4 × 15
Barbell Rowing	3 × 10	4 × 10
Bent-over One-arm Rowing	3 × 15	4 × 15
Standing Lateral Raises	3 × 15	5 × 10
Standing Front Raises	3 × 10	4 × 10
Barbell Triceps Press	3 × 15	4 × 15
Lying Triceps Press	3 × 15	4 × 15
Standing Dumbbell Curl	3 × 12	4 × 12
Barbell Curl	3 × 10	4 × 10
Forearm Wrist Curl	3 × 15	5 × 15
Calf Raises	4 × 15	6 × 15
Bench Sit-ups	3 × 30	4 × 30
Bench Leg Raises	3 × 30	4 × 30
Dips	1 × 10	2 × 10

Continue weight training on Monday, Wednesday, and Friday or on Tuesday, Thursday, and Saturday for the advanced program. Also continue using 7½-pound dumbbells and 2½-pound plates on your barbell. If you make rapid gains in strength during your first year on the advanced program you can change to 10-pound dumbbells and 5-pound plates. Consult your team coach before you use even heavier weights.

7

Weight Training for Your Favorite Team Sport

In any sport, the strongest player will have an advantage.

This is because strength is a basis for power and endurance. Strength also affects your balance, coordination, flexibility, speed, and quickness (reaction time). Added strength will improve even your agility—your ability to change directions while moving fast.

Physical strength is also important to the *mental* part of your game. Just knowing you are stronger and more powerful than your opponents will make a great difference in how well you play.

Think about strength.

Suppose that in a football game you are lined up against the opposing guard, tackle, or center. You have been training with weights for several years. You know you can deadlift a hundred pounds or more. You look at the opposing player. You size him up. You're sure you can move him, the same way you move all those pounds of iron weight. He may look bigger than you are. He may even look fierce. But you remember those many days in your gym lifting and lifting. You're confident. With the snap of the football you're ready to use the power you've worked hard for.

This confidence based on your strength is just as important in every other sport. In basketball you have confidence that late in the game you'll still be a strong jumper for blocking shots and capturing rebounds. In baseball you know right from "Play ball!" that the final innings will find you fresh at the plate, looking for a homer.

In all sports there are many things you can't control. Weather is one: A stormy day makes playing football difficult. You can't always control the quality of the baseball diamond or basketball court you must play on. You may end up falling on weedy base-paths or banging into the walls of a small,

Standing dumbbell clean and jerk (29A)

cramped gym. You can't control the abilities of your opponents or the skills of your teammates.

But you can control your own personal *fitness*. And the best single way to improve strength for sports is by lifting weights.

By the time you've been lifting for two or three months on the beginning program you're fit enough to add a few new exercises to your routine. In this chapter I've chosen five team sports. For each sport I've sug-

gested several exercises that will work on muscles you use in specific skills.

Like hitting a baseball. Your shoulder and chest muscles are the most important for hitting a baseball with power. Your deltoids and pectoralis muscles start the force that gets the ball under way. So an exercise to work these muscles extra hard is recommended.

This chapter is nothing like a complete guide to weight training for the five sports.

(29B)

I've suggested the exercises in this chapter mainly to start your own thinking for your favorite sport. You'll certainly want to read other books on the subject. Also you should talk to your coach to find out what exercises he suggests.

Now here's how to add these special exercises to your training program.

If you are at least two months along in the beginning program, add your sport ex-ercises to the *end* of your training schedule.

For example, if you are playing baseball this season, finish your ten beginning exercises, and then do your baseball exercises. A month or so before football season begins, add the football exercises to your schedule if you plan to play football, or the soccer exercises if you're going out for soccer.

As the sports seasons change you should add exercises and drop those for the sport you've finished playing. Continue to train

Jump squat (30)

with weights three times a week on your basic beginning, intermediate, or advanced schedule.

Exercise 29: Standing Dumbbell Clean and Jerk for Football

Strength is so important in football that coaches admit their best football players are almost always their best weight trainers!

This exercise builds explosive power in your whole body for the major actions on field: blocking, tackling, and running. Also you are increasing your joint flexibility, which helps prevent serious injuries.

Begin in position 29A. Hold your 5-pound dumbbell with both hands. Now swing it up to position 29B. Return to 29A and up again. Notice that your arm muscles, your shoulders, back, and legs are working together. Do 2 sets of 10.

During warm weather I often take my weights outside for a training session. I suggest you do that too sometimes for a change of pace. Keep your concentration by looking straight ahead, not back and forth at the scenery. You can gaze around when you're doing your warmdown stretches.

Exercise 30: Jump Squat for Soccer

Soccer is the world's most popular sport and is swiftly becoming a favorite in America. I've played soccer since my childhood. One skill I have had to work hard on is heading. Because I'm shorter than many of the players I go up against, I've had to learn an explosive jump to reach the soccer ball before my opponents.

This exercise is both easy and fun. Take a dumbbell in each hand. Now squat down and jump straight up. Regain your balance, squat, and jump again. If you do this 10 times at the end of every weight-training session you'll soon be out-heading taller boys on the soccer field.

Notice that with all the machines around I'm still using the basic beginning equipment—two dumbbells.

Exercise 31: Jumping Rope for Basketball

Jumping rope will develop the calves of your legs. That will mean greater leg spring in jumping for the basketball. Your rebounding and jump shooting will improve. Also your agility in other footwork.

You don't need any fancy rope-jumping steps like a prizefighter. Jump on the balls of your feet for a full minute. Take a break and jump for another minute. Gradually improve your endurance until you can jump three minutes without stopping for a rest. This way you are improving your running endurance on court.

Exercise 30 is also a good one for jump shooting and rebounding. Add both of these to your regular program.

Jumping rope (31)

Exercise 32: Dips for Baseball

Take a look around your neighborhood schools. One of them is bound to have a set of dip bars on the playground. If not, they're a lifetime investment for your home gym. For under $20.00 you'll have a piece of equipment that will give you a workout whenever you lift yourself up on them. In this exercise you are your own weight! Dips never become boring because they never become an easy exercise. They take power,

Dips (32A)

(32B)

Narrow grip chins (33)

Hanging
upside down (34)

balance, and coordination. The more you weigh, the harder they are.

Start in position 32A. Bend your arms, lowering your body slowly as far as possible. Pause at 32B and then push yourself back to 32A. Inhale while lowering your bodyweight, and exhale when recovering to the starting position.

Add power to your baseball swing by strengthening your pectoralis, deltoids, and triceps. Rest after each dip until in several months you can do 5–10 dips without resting in between.

Exercise 33: Narrow-grip Chins for Ice Hockey

Again, you are your own weight in chinning.

Using an underhand grip, hang from the

Further Exercises for Your Team Sports

Sport	*Exercise*	*Main Muscles Developed*	*Sport Skill Improved*
Football	Exercise 7 Standing Triceps Press	Triceps	Passing
Soccer	Exercise 25 Calf Raises	Calves	Kicking
Basketball	Exercise 8 Standing Dumbbell Curl	Biceps	Pulling ball away from opponent while rebounding
Baseball	Exercise 24 Forearm Wrist Curl	Wrist Flexors	Throwing
Ice Hockey	Exercise 1 Dumbbell Squat	Gluteus, Quadriceps	Skating

chinning bar just the way I'm hanging in 33. Pull your body upward so that your chin is resting on top of the bar. Lower yourself slowly. Pull again. Inhale while pulling up. Exhale on the way down.

Your latissimus dorsi muscles (lats) in the middle of your back are being strengthened. These muscles will give power to your shooting and checking. Build up each month so that you can do 5 chins in a row, then 10 chins in a row after several months.

Notice the position of my fingers. I spread them without hooking my thumb under the bar in order to spread my weight evenly on the muscles being worked. This prevents injuries and builds muscles faster.

Exercise 34: Hanging Upside Down

A good way to warm down after your workout is to hang upside down from the chinning bar. Hang loose. Breathe completely out.

A chinning bar is an inexpensive addition to your home gym.

Several weeks before the season begins, add one extra set of your sport's exercise to your regular program.

8

Weight Training for Popular Olympic Sports

Many of the boys I train with don't play team sports. They like individual sports instead. Some of them take private gymnastics lessons. Some ice skate and ski with their families on weekends. Others wrestle or box at the YMCA. And nowadays many boys run in distance races with their fathers and brothers.

No matter which individual sport you play you will probably want to improve. Even if you don't compete—if you play only for fun—you like to watch yourself get better. You want to try more complicated dives from higher boards. You want to ski longer, harder ski runs. You're hoping to swim faster and farther even though you're swimming around your own backyard pool.

If you compete in individual sports, you should know that the strongest athlete has the advantage.

As a competitor you've learned many skills in your sport. You've watched good athletes and imitated them. You've read books for new ideas. You have memorized tips you've heard from professionals on TV. You've studied pictures of the skills you need to work on, and you've practiced with the pictures in mind.

So far so good, because to improve in athletics you need to sharpen your skills. You must also strengthen your mental attitude—your desire. And of course you know by now you must strengthen your body.

You can learn *about* strength in the same way you learn *about* skills: by reading, watching, asking, and listening. You can find out which muscles you mainly use in your special sports. You can study pictures of weight-training exercises so you know exactly how to perform them.

But to improve your strength you can't simply watch. You have to work at it in the same way you work in the swimming pool on your butterfly stroke. To some extent your strength is improving as you practice any sport. In swimming, for example, the water is providing resistance. You are working against the water the way you work in your gym: water is the weight. And that's fine. Yet for even greater gains in strength—greater and faster gains—you should add weight training to your swimming program and to all your individual sports programs.

I want to explain skill and strength by giving an example of what I've written so far in this chapter. I'll use this story of a boy I trained with to show how his increased strength helped him become a winning runner.

Tom was cut from the junior-high football team because he was too small. He wanted to compete in some sport that fall, so when his dad suggested running in cross-country races. Tom gave it a try. He practiced the skills a racer needs: things like running on different surfaces (grass, sand, cement, etc.); running through water hazards; pacing himself over a 2-mile course. He practiced starting a race in a crowd and ending with a sprint and kick. He trained hard by running three miles a day, then four miles, and eventually five miles a day. He worked on his stride and on race tactics.

After Tom's first losses he asked me if I could help him run faster. We talked about how he felt after races. He confessed his arms always felt worse than his legs. But so what? He didn't run on his arms!

I started training with Tom on the beginning weight program. I also gave him some extra lifts for his arms and shoulders. These are very important in running. Your arms lead your legs. You pull with them. They help you set a rhythm. They help balance you. If your arms are tired, your running form becomes ragged, and you lose time swaying from side to side. Plus there's the mental factor: If your arms are tired in a race you are thinking, "My arms hurt," instead of thinking about your footplant, your pace, and your tactics.

Tom lifted weights to strengthen his shoulders and arms. He also did squats and calf raises to build up his legs. By the end of that season he was winning races. He looked forward to running the following spring on the track team after five more months of weight training combined with lots of distance running.

Lifting weights helped Tom's balance because strong arms stay in rhythm, while weak arms often flop and flap. His speed improved partly because strong shoulders and arms pull harder than weak ones can. Tom had the endurance that comes with physical and mental strength: After three miles of running, his arms felt fresher than they used to after half a mile. And his mind told his legs to run faster because he wasn't thinking about his hurting arms. He had the explosive power to pull his arms hard going up hill and swing them faster while sprinting the final yards to the tape.

For Tom, weights worked. And they will work for you.

Exercise 35: Wrist Curls with Barbell for Boxing

The first set of weights I ever owned was a pair of 2½-pound dumbbells. These were given to me to strengthen my punch. As an amateur boxer, I won 37 fights, with 22 knockouts. I still have my original dumbbells.

Wrist curls with a barbell are a variation on Exercise 24 in the intermediate program. Sit on a bench or chair with your elbows and forearms resting on your thighs. Flex your wrists, raising the barbell forward and upward. Pause and lower slowly to the starting position. Concentrate by watching your forearm muscles working.

Strong forearm flexors support your wrists so you can hold your boxing gloves at the proper level. Muscle endurance keeps your "dukes up" in the final minutes of each round when you're otherwise tired.

Use 2½-pound plates on your barbell for this exercise.

Another excellent weight exercise for

Wrist curls with barbell (35)

boxing is the incline barbell press (Exercise 38). If you take a little less than shoulder-width grip on the barbell your pressing action is close to the actual boxing punch.

To strengthen your punch even more: Take a 5-pound dumbbell in each hand and punch forward for 10 repetitions.

Exercise 36: Standing Dumbbell Curls for Running

Young runners pay little attention to their upper bodies. They train their legs with many miles of running and believe they've gone far enough to win races.

Chris knows better. Here he's doing an extra set of dumbbell curls on his begin-

Standing dumbbell curl (36)

Sit-ups (37A)

below, (37B)

Incline
barbell press
(38A)

(38B)

Running (39)

ning program. He's curling the dumbbells alternately for a change. Alternately or together, curls are building his biceps, those flexors that bend the arm.

During your next run, look down at your arms. If your thumbs are pointed straight ahead, as many coaches recommend, that means your arms are about half bent. Your biceps are helping to hold your arms steady on course.

Exercise 37: Bent Leg Situps for Diving and Swimming

When you look at pictures of divers you probably notice first their muscular legs.

Powerful leg action on the springboard is a key to successful diving. Looking at swimmers you're drawn to their muscular backs and chests. That's because arm pull is the main source of propulsion through water, and arm pull depends on the latissimus dorsi and pectoralis major.

Chris loves to dive and swim in pools around his neighborhood. When talking to him about how to improve, I suggested extra work on his abdominals. These aren't the muscles you would ordinarily think about in any sport, but for both diving and swimming they are crucial. Every competitive swimming stroke (free style, back crawl, breast stroke, butterfly) needs ab-

Lateral raises (40)

dominal strength for stabilizing your body in the water. Divers need well-toned abdominal muscles for twisting and bending movements in the air.

Bent leg situps begin in position 36A. Keep your hands interlocked behind your head and your feet flat on the floor. Sit up to 36B. Go all the way forward, until your head touches your knees. Then down. Take slightly longer to lower your body than to raise it. Your training partner can hold your feet on the floor. Or you can hook them under the legs of your bench.

Do 1 set of 10 in addition to the beginning program and 2 sets of 10 in addition to the bench situps on the intermediate program.

Exercise 38: Incline Barbell Press for Gymnastics

The pectoralis are two muscle groups in your chest: the pectoralis minor—smaller upper pectorals; and the pectoralis major—large lower pectorals. (See The Muscleman on pages 7–8.) These muscles move your upper arms forward. In gymnastics, pectoralis

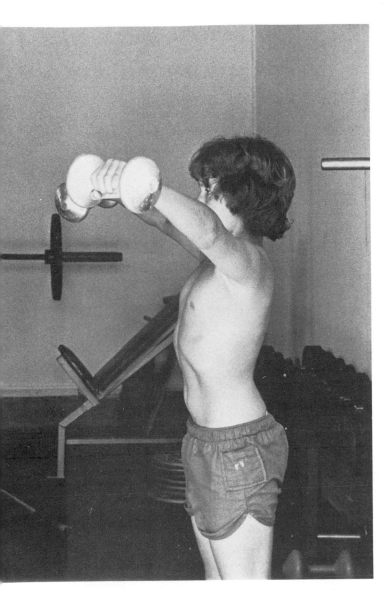

harder, ask your partner to hold your ankles. Then lower yourself. When you push back up your partner should offer resistance. He should pull your ankles gently down. That way you are lifting yourself *and* some of your partner's body weight.

Exercise 39: Running for Skating

Both kinds of Olympic skating, figure and speed, call for lower-body strength.

In summer when your usual ponds, lakes, and rivers aren't frozen for skating you can keep your legs in shape by running every day. Look for different kinds of running challenges: slight hills, steeper hills, flat tracks, sandy surfaces. Change your running course several times a month.

If you're a skater and have access to a leg machine (at the YMCA or at a health club), add two leg exercises to your program: leg extensions and leg curls. Do each of these with 10 pounds, 1 set of 10 repetitions. Work up to 3 sets of 10.

Exercise 40: Standing Lateral Raises for Skiing

Chris and I are working on his shoulder muscles for skiing. He needs deltoid strength for driving off his poles in both downhill and cross-country skiing.

You've been doing this exercise in your beginning program. Add an extra set of 10 repetitions about a month before you expect to start a new ski season. Raise the dumbbells sideward and upward so that they are parallel with your head. Pause and lower them to your starting position.

Exercise 41: Reverse Curl for Wrestling

Reverse curls work on the outer and upper parts of your forearms. These muscles flex and extend your hands. If you're a wrestler you already know the importance of a powerful and lasting grip. You know

strength is a must for pressing movements on the parallel bars and for the straight-arm lever you need in floor exercises.

Press the barbell to position 37B. Lower it slowly. Do 1 set of 10 at the end of your beginning program. Do 1 set of 10 just after your bench press on the intermediate program.

You can also do this exercise with a dumbbell in each hand. Hold them so your palms face away from your body.

Dips (Exercise 32) are especially right for gymnasts. As a variation to make dips

Reverse curl (41)

you use grip strength in all phases of wrestling.

Take a shoulder-width overgrip on the barbell. Stand straight with the barbell against your thighs. Curl the barbell up to your chin. Lower it slowly back against your thighs.

You may not be a wrestler, but almost every athlete gets into arm wrestling once in a while. To become a winner, train your forearms with extra reverse curls and wrist curls. Practice arm wrestling with your training partner. This will build your speed.

9

Weight Training for Weekend Sports

The weekend athlete is mostly having fun. He's bowling with friends on Friday nights and surfing with them on Saturday afternoons. He's hiking with his boy scout troop. He's skateboarding down to the store to pick up a quart of milk. He isn't especially trying to improve his sports. Although if it weren't too much trouble, he'd be willing to get better. No sweat. No strain.

Lifting weights to improve your sport is probably the easiest way to make sudden, dramatic progress. For the short time you give to the beginning program for overall strength (Chapter 4) you will see results in skateboarding, for example, that would take much longer by simply practicing skills. Lifting weights fewer than two hours a week will help you skateboard faster and with better moves and finesse, and you've never left your home gym to practice!

Sports improvement is not the only rea-son that a weekend athlete might have for training with weights.

He should also know that he is more susceptible to injury than is an athlete who practices his sport regularly. If the weekender keeps fit by lifting, he is less likely to strain a leg muscle or sprain an arm on Saturday. Many injuries happen because the athlete is tired. He gives in a little to his tiredness and that causes mistakes. Those mistakes lead to injuries. As I've said many times about weight lifting—it improves your muscles' endurance.

And I've also pointed out that just knowing you are strong affects the mental part of your weekend sport.

Let's take backpacking. It is one of the most mentally demanding sports. You *decide for yourself* how much effort you want to expend. You can decide to hike the steep mountain trails swiftly, stopping only at nightfall. Or you can walk slowly with

Standing barbell press (42)

many rests. Or you can sit in camp all day and dream about the high trails.

If you're physically strong you have the choice of hard, long-distance trails to places your friends will never see. You know your own power as you strap on your backpack. It's heavy with food, clothes, and your tent. But to you it feels light. You're used to lifting. You're sure you can hike twenty miles today. And if an emergency comes along—if you're lost—you'll remember your strength training. You'll stay calm. You'll know you have the endurance to make it safely home.

I train with boys who love the pure fun of weekend sports. They don't expect me to help them improve. Yet they do improve just by following the beginning, intermediate, or advanced programs and by adding a few extra lifts for the main muscle groups, the "prime movers" in their sports.

Exercise 42: Standing Barbell Press for Backpacking (Same as Exercise 11)

Legs, arms, shoulders, back—everything must be strengthened for hiking endurance, especially if you will be carrying a heavy pack over long distances. Experienced young hikers are able to carry 30–50 pounds over the trail for 20 miles a day.

This exercise works many muscles at the same time. Press the barbell from your chest to the overhead position. Return to the starting position and repeat, doing 1 set of 10 repetitions *in addition to* your intermediate program.

Forearm wrist curl (43)

Exercise 43: Forearm Wrist Curl for Bowling (Same as Exercise 24)

Bowling doesn't require the level of muscular development you need in gymnastics, wrestling, football, and in most other sports. But you do need strong forearms and hands to prevent fatigue during your final frames of the day. Such strength will help keep accuracy and consistency in your delivery.

Add an extra set of forearm wrist curls to your weight-training program. Also, keep a small rubber ball (a racquetball or handball is best) near the TV set. In the evening as you watch your favorite programs, squeeze the ball to build wrist muscles.

Exercise 44: Leg Extension for Skateboarding and Surfing

I've saved for this last chapter the leg

Leg extension (44)

Leg curl (45)

machine. As I've said throughout the book, you don't need any machine to build strength for athletics. You need nothing but the set of weights you've seen over and over in photographs so far.

But the leg machine is fun to use and makes a pleasant change in your training routines. And they aren't hard to find. Try your local YMCA. The high school in your district might let you come in to use their machine if they have one. It's worth your time to train on a leg machine at least once. If you like it, they cost very little to build for a home gym. You can use it to muscle up for skateboarding and surfing.

Leg muscles must be strong for the side-to-side and rotating moves on turns. If they aren't strong enough, you then are forced to pivot your hips and upper body, causing delayed turns. These cut down your fun because you don't have total confidence about controlling the board.

Sit on the extension machine. Lean back slightly, hands grasping the sides of the machine. Raise your legs until they are completely extended, pause, and lower to the starting position. Do not raise your buttocks off the bench. Don't bounce in any position. Do 2 sets of 10 repetitions.

Your quadriceps work hard on this machine.

Exercise 45: Leg Curl for Skateboarding and Surfing

Leg curls are done on the same machine as extensions.

Lie face down with your heels hooked under the roller. For comfort, your kneecap should be just off the edge of the pad. Raise your lower legs until they are a foot higher than mine in position 44. Pause and return to the starting position. Keep your upper body flat on the table.

This machine works your hamstring muscles. Do 2 sets of 10 repetitions. Enjoy sitting down for a change while exercising.

**Lift for strength and health.
Lift to win.
Lift for life.**

Index